Recessional—Or,
the Time of the Hammer

Tom McCarthy

**Recessional—Or,
the Time of the Hammer**

Edited by Elisabeth Bronfen

diaphanes

Series **THINK ART** of the Institute for Critical Theory (ith) –
Zurich University of the Arts and the Centre for Arts and
Cultural Theory (ZKK) – University of Zurich.

1st edition
ISBN 978-3-03734-589-4
© diaphanes, Zurich-Berlin 2016
All rights reserved.

Layout: 2edit, Zurich
Printed in Germany

www.diaphanes.com

Contents

Tom McCarthy

**Recessional—Or,
the Time of the Hammer**

Towards the end of Thomas Pynchon's mammoth
1973 novel *Gravity's Rainbow*, the stumbling ingénue
of a hero Tyrone Slothrop sets off on a commando
raid. The territory he and his cohorts move through
is a giant metropolis, a "factory-state" in which capital, technology and power, perfectly co-calibrated,
send airships drifting through urban canyons, past
chrome caryatids and roof-gardens on skyscrapers
that themselves shoot up and down on elevator-cables:
a conurbation Pynchon calls the "City of the Future"
or "Raketen-Stadt." The raid's target, though, is not a
building; nor is it a person; it is, rather, time. Slothrop
has been dispatched to rescue "the Radiant Hour,"
which associates of a villain known only as "the Father" have "abstracted from the day's 24." As Slothrop,
suiting up and setting out, is handed a note informing
him, in matinee adventure style: "The Radiant Hour is
being held captive, if you want to see her...," the bul-
lets zinging past his head "conveniently" give over to a
clock face, drifting, like the airships, through the sky.

How do we digest or get a bearing on this bizarre
episode? The fact that one of the "Floundering Four"
commandos is a "very serious-looking French refugee
kid" named Marcel, "a mechanical chess-player dating

back to the Second Empire" given to long-winded monologues, might point us towards Proust, inviting us to view Slothrop's escapade as a reworking of that other raid on lost (or misappropriated) time, stage-managed by a writer who has put something extra in his *madeleines*. The intention was probably there on Pynchon's part—yet as I re-read the sequence a few weeks ago, my mind kept drifting (maybe it was the Franco-Germanic mix of Marcel and Raketen-Stadt, the general elevation of the setting) to another scene, another half-occluded precedent; one that plays out, like this evening's talk, in Switzerland.

Thomas Mann's equally-mammoth work *The Magic Mountain* announces, right from the outset, an obsession with time. As Hans Castorp (another ingénue protagonist) winds his way up through mountains to the Davos sanatorium to visit his tubercular cousin, the space through which his train chuffs starts to take on "the powers we generally ascribe to time." Numerous temporal meditations follow—on duration, on persistence, continuity, recurrence. As though foreseeing that Davos would become the seat of the World Economic Forum, Mann has one of Hans's teachers, Naphta, explain the global financial market to him as a temporally-grounded system, a mechanism for "receiving a premium for the passage of time—interest, in other words." At the outset of a chapter titled "By the Ocean of Time," the form and very possibility of the book we are reading become similarly index-linked to time, "For time is the medium of narration." "Can one tell—that is to say, narrate—time, time itself, as such, for its own sake?" Mann wonders. No: "That would surely be an absurd undertaking." Yet he concedes that any narrative contains two kinds of time: that of its actual time, the time it takes to iterate itself; and that of its content, which is "extremely relative," such that a narrative that concerned itself with the events of five minutes might take up hundreds of hours, and, conversely, the contents of a moment's iteration might expand beyond "the extreme limit of man's temporal capacity for experience." The latter, expansive instances, he claims, are possessed of "a morbid element" and are akin to opium dreams in which "something had been taken away" from the brain of the sleeper, "like the spring from a broken watch."

Hans plans to stay at the sanatorium for three weeks; but, himself diagnosed with TB on arrival, is held up there for seven years. His illness not only forces an extended delay, time off from his work as an engineer, a general time-out from his life; it also imposes its own temporality. When you are ill in bed, Mann writes,

> All the days are nothing but the same day repeating itself—or rather, since it is always the same day, it is incorrect to speak of repetition; a continuous present, an identity, an everlastingness—such words as these would better convey the idea. They bring you your midday broth, as they brought it yesterday and will bring it tomorrow; and it comes over you—but whence or how you do not know, it makes you quite giddy to see the broth coming in—that you are losing a sense of the demarcation of time, that

its units are running together, disappearing; and what is being revealed to you as the true content of time is merely a dimensionless present in which they eternally bring you the broth.

Colored by shades of eternity and entropy or run-down, illness-time is time that is drifting towards death. But it is also, in classic Freudian fashion, time that is homing in on pleasure. Illness "makes men more physical," Mann notes; racking women's frames, consumption brings about a "heightening and accentuation" of their curves and outlines, turns them into beings "exaggerated by disease and rendered twice over body." "Phthisis and concupiscence go together," remarks Dr. Behrens, while his colleague Dr. Krokowski talks of love, forced underground by "fear, conventionality, aversion, or a tremulous yearning to be pure," re-emerging "in the form of illness. Symptoms of disease are nothing but a disguised manifestation of the power of love; and all disease is only love transformed."

These lines of thought play out dramatically (as those of you who have read the book will know) in the relation between Hans and fellow patient Claudia Chauchat (her name, beside denoting femininity and lust, is also that of a make of machine-gun). Hans experiences his desire for her as an extension and intensification of his illness. In a gesture that redeems a romantic cliché by literalizing it, Mann has Hans's temperature, constantly thermometer-gauged, rise two notches every time he sees her; and, in a similar materialization of chivalric code, he makes him carry around an X-ray of her lungs, pressed tight against his chest: thus she becomes, like Pynchon's stolen hour, both radiant and negative, abstracted. Though she remains beyond his reach for virtually the whole novel, he mounts a seduction in the book's central episode, which takes place on Walpurgis Night—a festival or holiday abstracted even from the abstracted life of the sanatorium, time out of the time-out ("almost," as Hans puts it, "outside the calendar, intercalated, so to speak, a twenty-ninth of February"). The seduction sequence begins with him re-enacting (unbeknown to Claudia) another episode that shaped his childhood when, aged thirteen, he borrowed a pencil from a boy on whom he had a crush. Recalling the childhood incident earlier in the novel has already caused him to be rapt back into the past "so strongly, so resistlessly" that his present body has seemed like that of a cadaver "while the actual Hans Castorp moved in that far-away time and place"; replaying it on Walpurgis Night as he asks Claudia for her pencil places him, once more, "on the tiled court of the schoolyard."

Thus a complex, spring-like structure opens up, stretching and contracting such that quite separate moments touch or get embedded one within the other, with a synecdoche or marker for the act of writing (the pencil) running through it all. Lavishing praise on Claudia's flesh "destinée pour l'anatomie du tombeau," Hans asks to die with his lips pressed to hers. Most commentaries on *The Magic Mountain* interpret the fact that Claudia leaves the party at this point as a rebuff; yet her words in the doorway—"*N'oubliez pas de me rendre mon crayon*"—Hans's pointedly late return to his own room, and Mann's mention of more words exchanged between them that night at "a later interval, wordless to our ears, during which we have elected to intermit the flow of our story along the stream of time, and let time flow on pure and free of any content whatever" strongly suggest the opposite. If it is the writing implement that opens the approach to death-like pleasure up, though, it is the same one that, in Mann's hands, places its consummation in a blind spot. Either way, content-time kicks back in the next day, and Claudia leaves, returning much later as the companion of the older Mynheer Peeperkorn, who, standing between Hans and her, becomes one more of Hans's surrogate fathers. Peeperkorn will commit suicide, while Hans, discharged, is sent off to the front of World War One, as the novel's ironic ending sees the long, intimate, death-like intermission of the sanatorium give over to the wholesale mechanized slaughter of historical progression.

*

Hans Castorp, of course, isn't the only literary hero with TB. We could all probably name a handful of writers who succumbed to it, and scores more characters. One of this second group whose story doesn't get discussed so much these days, not least because of the racist epithet in its title, is the hero of Joseph Conrad's novella *The Nigger of the Narcissus*. The setting (for those of you who need reminding) is a British Merchant vessel sailing back to London from Bombay—a little world, just like Mann's sanatorium, with its hierarchies and operational rhythms, isolated from the larger one it micro-mirrors, set this time at a degree zero of elevation, on a literal ocean. As the first mate calls the roster prior to casting off, and notes that they are one man short (there is an extra name written down there, but he can't make it out; it is smudged), he is about to dismiss the crew when a voice calls out: "Wait!" The mate, incensed by the insubordination, demands to know who dared to tell *him* to wait—whereupon a black man steps out of the shadows, a West Indian sailor named James Wait.

No sooner has Wait announced his presence than a cough leaps from him, "metallic, hollow, and tremendously loud; it resounded like two explosions in a vault; the dome of the sky ran to it, and the iron plates of the ship's bulwarks seemed to vibrate in unison." He will spend most of the trip laid up with his coughing; on the rare occasions when he steps out on deck, "a black mist emanated from him... something cold and gloomy that floated out and settled on all the faces like a mourning veil." Conrad heaps funereal symbols (corpses, coffins, shrouds) upon Wait; and Wait welcomes the association, telling the crew he is dying at every opportunity, even seeming "to take a pride in that death." "He would," writes Conrad, "talk of that coming death as though it had been already there, as if it had been walking the deck outside, as if it would presently come in to sleep in the only empty bunk; as if it had sat by his side at every meal." The effect on the crew is complex. Wait's morbidity fills them with trepidation, while his black face repulses them. At the same time, his plight awakens their humanity. They indulge him; cover for him; bring him meals, even plunder the ship's supplies to pander to him. Before long, they become loyal yet dread-filled servants, "the base courtiers of a hated prince." The forecastle in which they lodge him turns into a "church" where men, entering, speak only "in low tones"—or, in more pagan shades, a "shrine where a black idol, reclining stiffly under a blanket, blinked its weary eyes and received our homage." "He had the secret of life, that confounded dying man, and he made himself master of every moment of our existence."

But is he genuine? In an exchange with his fellow crewmember Donkin, a work-shy syndicalist whose shirking has nothing of the metaphysical about it (Conrad's novella is decidedly not tailored to a liberal readership), Wait admits to "shamming" his sickness in order to obtain an easy passage. And yet even as he speaks the words, more coughs rattle his by-now skeletal frame. When the captain accuses him of shamming too (as it turns out, from compassion—he, like the rest of them, can see that Wait is doomed), Wait claims to have recovered; the captain confines him to his forecastle, and the crew almost mutiny. Yet the stand-off seems more philosophical than political: Wait's "steadfastness to his untruthful attitude" (a double-edged term, since Wait is lying twice over: lying about being well, and lying about lying in the first place) "in the face of the inevitable truth had," writes Conrad, "the proportions of a colossal enigma." The whole ship teeters on the edge of an abysmal ambiguity; "nothing in her was real." It drifts into the doldrums, which (since it is sail-powered) delays its onward passage—a hiatus that seems to affirm that "The universe conspired with James Wait," since he, too, as he drifts deathwards, is borne into "regions of memory that know nothing of time." "There was," writes Conrad, "something of the immutable quality of eternity in the slow moments of his complete restfulness." And, as in *The Magic Mountain*, lurking somewhere in the depths of this un-clockworked death-space is a half-buried scene of sexual pleasure: in his delirium, Wait mumbles about a "Canton Street girl... She chucked a third engineer of a Rennie boat... for me. Cooks oysters just as I like..."

After he finally dies and disappears, canvas-wrapped, into the sea, the wind picks up and the Narcissus speeds onwards to London. The last scene sees the crew collect their pay (Wait's own salary, since he has no claimants, is put aside, retained) in the shipping company's office just beside the Royal Mint—for a merchant ship's passage is, after and above all, a move in the great monetary game of industry and trade. Yet, under the name of Wait, a dark aporia has opened up somewhere inside the game-space; a suspension or negation of its logic; a threat, or at least the kernel of one, to its very continuation.

*

As I wrote this lecture, I kept hearing a tune playing in my head, as you do. It was a particular tune, repeating over and over again: MC Hammer's "U Can't Touch This." You know the one: it is built around a single four-beat musical phrase that loops round and round, while MC Hammer overlays the verbal phrases "U Can't Touch this" and "Stop! Hammertime." How logical is the Unconscious. This was no random, meaningless distraction: the song couldn't have been more germane to the thoughts I was trying to piece together—for doesn't it, like Conrad's novella, feature a black man who tells us to wait? A little detective work, the kind you can easily do on Wikipedia, reveals the repeating tune to already be a repetition: MC Hammer has sampled it from Rick James's "Superfreak," removing James's lyrics ("She's a very kinky girl/The kind you don't take home to mother") and inserting his refrain "U Can't touch this" in the little pause, the suspended beat that opens just before the tune loops round again. We get this opening refrain three times; then, in the "break-down" coda separating one verse from the next, its rejoinder: "Stop! Hammertime"—as though, just like Wait, Hammer were baptizing the hiatus with his own name.

Conrad's novella was first published, in 1897, with a preface that is generally taken as the author's overriding literary manifesto. Drawing an analogy between the manual laborer and the writer, Conrad calls the latter a "worker in prose"—but, counterintuitively, links the great literary work not to a labor's successful completion, but rather to its suspension. "To arrest, for the space of a breath, the hands busy about the work of the earth, and compel men entranced by the sight of distant goals to glance for a moment at the surrounding vision of form and color, of sunshine and shadows; to make them pause for a look, for a sigh, for a smile—such is the aim, difficult and evanescent, and reserved only for a very few to achieve." *Arrest* and *pause* are the key terms here; also *reserved*, which conveys the sense of some great bounty or reward that, like Wait's salary (or Claudia, or the Radiant Hour), has been withheld, removed to a location beyond normal reach. Conrad's preface, for all its talk of pauses and arrests, is equally spatial: the writer "descends within himself, and in that lonely region of stress and strife, if he be deserving and fortunate, he finds the terms of his appeal." That the descent into and re-emergence from this dark region "binds the dead to the living" by holding up a "rescued fragment" of truth to the light gives it a thoroughly Orphic character—and turns the entire preface, for me, into a kind of dry-run for that seminal twentieth-century literary manifesto that Maurice Blanchot would publish 50 years later under the title "The Gaze of Orpheus." I have written about this at some length elsewhere, so will confine myself to noting here that Blanchot carries Conrad's motifs of arrest and incompletion one step further: what's remarkable about Orpheus, he points out, is not that he manages to rescue the lost radiant object, but that (in looking back) he interrupts and vandalizes even his own labor, bringing back to the light not Eurydice's presence but rather her absence.

This logic of the negative pervades all Blanchot's work. As though also thinking of "hands busy about the work of the earth," he writes: "Take the trouble to listen to a single word: in that word, nothingness is struggling and toiling away, it digs tirelessly, doing its best to find a way out, nullifying what encloses it"—this in an essay called "Literature and the Right to Death." No writer is more death-obsessed than Blanchot; and, for him, death is intimately tied in with the question of time. His short novella *Death Sentence*, also utterly Orphic, narrates an encounter between a man and his dead female friend whose corpse he visits, during which visit, despite remaining quite dead, she sits up and chats casually with him—for a while. Its original French title, *L'Arrêt de Mort*, contains the double sense of a condemnation *and* a temporary reprieve or suspension (an *arrête*), as though the judge's hammer hovered in mid-air above its block. His later, auto-biographical essay *L'Instant de ma Mort* recounts his experience of facing a firing squad during the Second World War—feeling, despite everything, a rush of joy as the soldiers, "in an immobility that arrested time," pointed their guns at him; then, when the actual shooting inexplicably failed to happen (he would live another sixty years), a perpetual sense of carrying "the instant of my death henceforth always in abeyance"— *L'instant de ma mort désormais toujours en instance*. Writing of death elsewhere, he distinguishes *le mort*, death itself, from *mourir*, dy-*ing*: where the first would be a thing that one could grasp, experience, consume (an unrealizable fantasy—yet one that underlies the entire tragic and Romantic literary traditions), the second is a neutral, uncontainable, un-masterable drifting, a movement of absenting. Thus, for the Blanchot of *The Writing of the Disaster*, dying is the opposite of death: it is "the incessant imminence whereby life lasts, desiring."

Dy-*ing*, desir-*ing*: in grammatical terms, these nonfinite verbs belong to the gerund—the form that, in English, also serves as the present participle. The tense, if you like, of Hans Castorp's eternally arriving soup. Or, to take another high-modernist literary instance, of Addie Bundren's passage through the novel whose very title contains Blanchot's gerund: *As I Lay Dying*. This work contains or concentrates so many of the processes and motifs we've been looking at this evening. Not only does Addie, like Wait, slowly and languorously die, but the hiatus mushrooms outwards even after the death-moment: while her family transport her coffin to the burial place she has stipulated, encountering delays at every step, the corporeality that Mann associates with illness is taken to its own zero degree as her rotting corpse draws buzzards from the sky and sends townspeople running gagging from its path. Advancing "with a motion so soporific, so dreamlike as to be uninferant of progress," the family edge towards a flooded river, and Addie's son Darl muses, in a gesture that will be familiar: "It is as though the space between us were time: an irrevocable quality." He continues: "It is as though time, no longer running straight before us in a diminishing line, now runs parallel between us like a looping string, the distance being the doubling accretion of the thread." It is into this accretion that Addie's body threatens to disappear as the flood waters sweep the coffin from the cart. But Darl rescues it—and a few pages later, in the novel's most extraordinary sequence, Faulkner gives the dead Addie her own monologue; Eurydice, rather than Orpheus, speaks.

She speaks both in and of the negative. "I learned," she says, "that words are no good; that words don't ever fit even what they are trying to say at." Even the word *love* "is just a shape to fill a lack." Lying beside her husband Anse, who has tricked her by hiding inside that last word,

> I would think about his name until after a while I could see the word as a shape, a vessel, and I would watch him liquefy and flow into it like cold molasses flowing out of the darkness into the vessel, until the jar stood full and motionless: a significant shape profoundly without life like an empty door frame; and then I would find that I had forgotten the name of the jar.

Anse is, she tells us, dead; her revenge on him consists in not letting him know that, and her marital bond in the fact "that I did not even ask him for what he could have given me: not-Anse. That was my duty to him, to not ask that, and that duty I fulfilled. I would be I; I would let him be the shape and echo of his word." Her affair with the pastor Whitfield is conducted largely in the hope that the Christian schema of sin and subsequent redemption will act as a funnel "to shape and coerce" the "terrible blood" of existence into a form of presence and equivalence, but since divinity itself is just "the forlorn echo of the dead word high in the air" (and "salvation is just words too"), the affair ends—which places her inside a kind of timelessness in which "to me there was no beginning nor ending to anything." And occupying this space, this temporality, she tells us in a fascinating turn of phrasing, "I even held Anse refraining still, not that I was holding him recessional..."

These words need some unpacking. *Refraining* is the more straightforward: I take it to mean that she is holding herself back from revealing Anse to himself as the not-Anse that, to her, he more profoundly is-maintaining him, to use the kind of photographic diction X-ray-clasping Hans Castorp might understand, in false-positive mode by keeping out of sight the actual negative from which this positive is (again and again, an ongoing illusion) printed. *Recessional* is more complex though. The OED gives *recessional* as: "1. Of or belonging to the recession or retirement of the clergy and choir from the chancel to the vestry at the close of a service; esp. *recessional hymn*, a hymn sung while this retirement is taking place. 2. Belonging to a recess (of Parliament)." *Recess*, in turn, is given (inter alia) as "The act of retiring, withdrawing, or departing... a period of cessation from usual work or employment... a place of retirement, a remote, secret or private place... a niche or alcove... to place in a recess or in retirement; to set back or away..." It is a long entry, spanning architectural, juridical, anatomical and a host of other contexts—not least economic (aren't we now living through a recession?). If Addie *is* holding Anse refraining, *recessional* describes the manner in which she is *not* holding him, names the inner sanctum into which she is denying him entry (can't touch this), the time-out-of-time that will never be measured on his clock-face, governed by his legislature—and, in so doing, names the suspended or abstracted beat around whose absence the whole mechanism of the book is orchestrated. *As I Lay Dying*, for all its entropy and breakdown, is a neatly circular novel in which all actions come back round as the cycle of life rotates: Addie's son Cash breaks the same leg twice, her daughter Dewey Dell gets screwed over (or screwed) twice, and so forth; and Anse, in the final punch line, marries the woman from whom he borrowed the spade he has just dug Addie's grave with. The corpse may be disposed of, the cycle restarted, but the recess has staked its claim right at its core, carved out its niche at twelve o'clock of midnight and high noon.

*

A pattern is, I hope, emerging here. If I have been drawing on works that, despite their evident preoccupation with issues of race and gender, were all authored by white men, this is not simply from a placid conservatism. Rather, it is an attempt to tease out (draw into the light, Conrad would say) a rationale, or counter-rationale, working both in and, perhaps, against literature's very canon. That the texts all come from the high-modernist period is no coincidence either—for isn't that when an exponentially accelerating industrialization, its accompanying technologies and ideologies, not only consolidated their claim (staked at least a century earlier) as the prime subject of literature and art but also radically reshaped its forms? Perhaps I'm hoping, in some paranoid (Pynchon-influenced) way, for a *Eureka!* instant; hoping to unearth a codex, a Rosetta Stone that would decode this moment and its legacy, both outside of and within—even *as*—literature. That, of course, is as much a fantasy as the Romantic/tragic one of owning one's own death: there is no single codex. But, I'd suggest, the closest thing we're going to get to one is the corpus of Mallarmé. Not only did he break form down until it reached its own zero degree; he carried out this overhaul as part of an ongoing and active theorization of literature itself. As Derrida points out, whatever else Mallarmé seems to be describing, he is always also writing about the operation *of* writing, feeling his way around the contours of the book-to-come, the *livre* to which everything is destined to belong. I've argued elsewhere that without Mallarmé there would be no Joyce; and the same could be said of everyone from William Burroughs to John Cage. Barthes summed up twentieth-century literary activity by saying: "All we do is repeat Mallarmé—but if it's Mallarmé we repeat, we do right." How much more relevant, then, is the great thinker of the "virtual," of total legibility and omni-data, to the twenty-first?

A million things could be said about Mallarmé and the subject still be barely breached. And we have only a few minutes left—so let's, by way of sketching out a much, much larger conversation to be had, home straight in on this fact: that Mallarmé is obsessed with the question of the pause, the interval, the recess. In a sketch from *Divagations* that seems to rehearse, to a *T,* Conrad's scene of interrupted labor, he presents workmen, "artisans of elementary tasks," taking a break from digging, lying around in such a manner as to "honorably reserve the dimension of the sacred in their existence by a work stoppage, an awaiting, a suicide." In an 1885 letter to Verlaine he writes:

> In the final analysis, I consider the contemporary era to be a kind of interregnum for the poet, who has nothing to do with it: it is too fallen or too full of preparatory effervescence for him to do anything but keep working, with mystery, so that later, or never, and from time to time sending the living his calling card—some stanza or sonnet—so as not to be stoned by them if they knew he suspected that they didn't exist.

An extraordinary formulation: the poet, occupying the interregnum, is dead—by implication, since he's differentiated from "the living" to whom he sends his calling card (the work). But, in so doing, he refrains from giving the lie to the pretence of their existence—in other words, and at the risk of being not just once but twice dead (stoned, martyred), the poet plays the role of Addie Bundren. Plays it from the recess: another passage in *Divagations* pictures Villiers de L'Isle Adam, his great tome forever kept from sight, withheld, reserved, knocking at the front door "like the sound of an hour missing from clock faces":

> Midnights indifferently thrown aside for his wake, he who always stood beside himself, and annulled time as he talked: he waved it aside as one throws away used paper when it has served its function; and in the lack of ringing to sound a moment not marked on any clock, he appeared…

Yet this timeless appearance, "from the point of view of History," is not "untimely" but "punctual"—for, Mallarmé continues, "it is not contemporary with any epoch, not at all, that those who exalt all significa-tion should appear"; they are both "projected several centuries ahead" and "turned toward the past." Both poetry and history demand such an appearance, *and* at the same time find themselves quite at a loss to locate it within their own parameters, their bounds or measures. In *Action Restrained* this situation takes on a distinctly political hue. We are, Mallarmé tells us, as he sketches a Pynchonesque scenario of rapid transit though some great metropolis, approaching a tunnel, "the epoch," a "forever time":

> time unique in the world, since because of an event I have still to explain, there is no Present, no—a present does not exist… Lack the Crowd declares in itself, lack—of every-thing. Ill-informed anyone who would announce himself his own contemporary, deserting, usurping with equal

impudence, when the past ceased and when a future is slow to come, or when both are mingled perplexedly to cover up the gap ... So watch out and be there.

There is, in the offing, lurking, "pulsing in the unknown womb of the hour," an *event*—yet one that cannot name itself, nor even find a solid time-platform to arise and stand on. No wonder Badiou turns to Mallarmé when he wants to elucidate his core or signature concept: the event, which, standing on the edge of the void so as to interpose itself between the void and itself (another doubling accretion), has "no acceptable ontological matrix." Calling up the "eternal circumstances" of the shipwreck in *A Throw of the Dice*, Badiou calls Mallarmé "a thinker of the event-drama, in the double sense of the staging of its appearance–disappearance":

> every event, apart from being localized by its site, initiates the latter's ruin *with regard to the situation*, because it retroactively names its inner void. The 'shipwreck' alone gives us the allusive debris from which (in the one of the site) the undecidable multiple of the event is composed.

Fine. But what would Mallarmé's un-named event *be*? Political revolution? Poetic epiphany? As Badiou points out, the central verb in *A Throw of the Dice*, the one around which the whole text turns, is *hésite*: the master's dice-clasping hand, poised above the waves, holds back (like that of Blanchot's judge) from leaping into action, from descending to unleash the decisive cast. The only name that we could really give this "un-decidable multiple" is Wait.

Derrida, too, turns at a key point in the trajectory of his thinking to Mallarmé—specifically, to the short text *Mimique* (which has been variously translated as "Dumb-show," "Mime," "Mimicry" and "Mimesis"). There, contemplating a mime-artist whose degree-zero corporeality renders his body both tool and subject of his performance, Mallarmé claims that what is illustrated is

> but the idea, not any actual action, in a Hymen (out of which flows Dream), tainted with vice yet sacred, between desire and fulfillment, penetration and remembrance; here anticipating, there recalling, in the future, in the past, *under the false appearance of a present*. That is how the mime operates, whose act is confined to a perpetual allusion without breaking the ice in the mirror: he thus sets up a medium, a pure medium, of fiction.

Derrida, of course, homes straight in on the *between*, hearing in Mallarmé's *entre* the *antra* of a cave or grotto, the *antara* of an interval. "What counts here," he writes, "is the *between*, the in-between-ness of the hymen"—symbol of marital union (Addie's and Anse's, for example) *and* membrane denoting separateness, through which "difference without presence appears, or rather baffles the process of appearing, by dislocating any orderly time at the center of the present." It is this baffling dislocation that sets up the "pure medium of fiction." *Fiction* would not be un-truth, as in Wait's lie or double-lie, or Addie's systematic pretence; nor would it be story, in Mann's sense of the unfolding of a narrative around temporal flow; rather, it would be recessionality itself. Fiction would be Hammertime.

Between. In *A Throw of the Dice*, in the long pause initiated by the master's frozen gesture, a figure appears, feather—or pen—in cap: Hamlet, Western literature's most celebrated avatar of hesitation. Everyone and everything in that play is suspended: between order and execution, word and deed, heaven and hell. Even death is recessive: Hamlet wishes for its consummation but sees only continuity, the gerund—which, of course, gives him pause; Polonius's body starts to rot and smell under the staircase; the passage of Ophelia's into the ground is interrupted. Re-reading it recently, I was struck by the number of times *Julius Caesar* was knowingly alluded to within its pages (an unusual move for Shakespeare)—which, in turn, sent me back to Brutus's complaint about his own restless delay:

> Since Cassius first did whet me against Caesar,
> I have not slept.
> Between the acting of a dreadful thing
> And the first motion, all the interim is
> Like a phantasma, or a hideous dream:
> The Genius and the mortal instruments
> Are then in council; and the state of man,
> Like to a little kingdom, suffers then
> The nature of an insurrection.

Acting, here, means (once more) the precise opposite of action: it means the conception of the action to be done, and the foundation of the baffling interim that both conjoins this to and separates this from its consummation, its "first motion." *Like a phantasma, or a hideous dream*. Tool-downage, implements (*instruments*) idle, waiting. In this most political of plays, this recess is called *council*, and man's being a *state … a little kingdom*. Yet what's truly revolutionary (in all senses of the word) here is *not* the putative end goal, the murder of the Emperor or overthrow of state; it is the interim itself. *Then* is the time where insurrection lurks: *then … then*—he says it twice, the temporal qualifier doubles or accretes, as though to open up and ground its referent: the interim, interim-time. And that, as we know, is the time of fiction.

"Obsessed with buffering"
Questions to Tom McCarthy

Elisabeth Bronfen

We're going to see whether we have some questions. Good, I don't even have to break the ice.

Audience

The icebreaking fits well because I think I have another work for your collection: *The Rime of the Ancient Mariner* by Coleridge. It's a voyage to the South Pole—so hence the ice—but I was thinking of the fact that Coleridge frames the story that the ancient mariner tells with a sinful act. That sinful act is of course shooting the albatross. This then brings on the suspension of time which moves the ship into the Doldrums. Nothing moves anymore, everybody dies and then the ghost ship turns up with Death and Life throwing the dice for the soul of the ancient mariner. Death loses so the ship continues with the whole crew who are basically zombies: dead bodies that are moved around by supernatural creatures. The ship sales back to England and the moment it reaches the harbor, everybody drops dead, the ship falls apart and the only person who survives is the ancient mariner who is now condemned to tell his story.

Tom McCarthy

"He stoppeth one of three" outside a church where a wedding is going to happen.

Audience

That's right, he stops them on the way to the consummation of the wedding. Do you agree that this fits the general narrative of your talk?

T.MC.

Yes, absolutely. There's another wonderful ship moment in *Dracula* as well on the *Demeter:* they're dead or they're all going to die—or more precisely, they're *transporting* death, undead death (Dracula), in a coffin, just like Addie Bundren. I always think this is somehow about September the 11th: the last ones to die crash the ship into the harbor; with their last strength they just tie themselves to the steering wheel and head straight for the town rather than the designated parking space—which on September the 11th would be the airport. There seems to be something very prescient about this death ship driven by someone who is already effectively dead.

I had forgotten about the dice in the *Ancient Mariner*, but the point in Mallarmé is that the dice is not thrown, although the poem itself produces a dicey numbering of some type.

Audience

But I think that that would be my point: this is probably the difference between a Romantic poem and a

Modernist poem. In Romanticism what we need is the allegory, what we need is the sin and what we need is the actual gamble, whereas in Modernism it's all about suspending.

T.MC.

Yes, and this is also what Beckett is all about. The event can't happen and if it did that would be redemption: "We'll be saved, if he just turns up we'll be saved." But Godot doesn't turn up and they just re-enact the interval again and again while it gets bigger and worse—in *Endgame* even the clock is breaking.

Audience

I'll give you another text and I also have a question. Another text would simply be *Frankenstein*. The whole of the *Frankenstein* novel takes place because they're locked in ice. So the waiting time, which is the frame narrative, is in fact also the writing time and the narration time.

T.MC.

Yes, he writes to kill time because he's bored; he's stuck in ice. I've always thought that *Frankenstein* is actually a novel about incest. It's about machine culture and incest.

Audience

I think it's about many things.

Principally I'm convinced this is what's going on in that book. Byron gives his maiden speech in parliament in defense of the machine breakers—the Luddites—who were all being put out of work by computers basically, by knitting machines. It's a capital offense to break a machine in England at this point and Byron, a hereditary peer, stands up and says, "these guys are great." And he's also having an affair with his half sister and scandalizing everyone and he turns up on lake Geneva. And in the book, Walter, who is stuck in ice, is writing to his sister and Frankenstein the inventor is meant to marry his kind-of sister. The monster kills the sister after the wedding, but before they've consummated it. So the monster is "good" there: he's being the super-ego and stopping the true horror of incest from taking place. But then the monster turns up and says to him that Frankenstein has to make him (the monster) a sister that *he* can marry and procreate with. And while Frankenstein is making a sister-monster, he becomes so appalled by the possibility of incest that he literally rips the female monster apart. There's a brilliant Warhol–Morrissey reprise of that in the film *Flesh for Frankenstein* where, at that moment, the inventor gets sexually aroused and has sex with the female monster through a wound where he's just sewn all the organs in. Then he turns to his Hollywood-cliché assistant with the hunchback and says, "to know death, Otto, you must fuck life in the gall bladder."

Audience

To come back to my question: you talk about the political, you talk about the aesthetic, you emphasize yourself that most of the texts you've invoked are high Modernist and we're playing some Romantic texts into this discussion as well. I'm curious to know in what way your interest in this question of suspended time with the interval—perhaps that's the moment of the real—fits into where we are right now. I'm thinking of Jonathan Crary's book *24/7* and of this idea that as people living we are constantly awake. No one ever sleeps and everyone is exhausted because precisely the moment you are talking about, the idea of suspended time with intervals of an in-between and the idea of pausing, is something that our culture is almost destructive of at the moment. So is this—your talk—nostalgia?

T.MC.

No, this is an archeology of the present. Like I said just after you introduced me, I've become obsessed with buffering—or the narrator in my new novel is obsessed with buffering. He's an anthropologist who has grown up reading Lévi-Strauss but he's also a *corporate* anthropologist who is working for the Man. He's putting culture in the service of capital. Like we all do, he spends most of his life staring at a screen, and he frequently encounters bouts of buffering. And the first thought he has is that this is not ultimately a technological situation, it's a theological situation. Behind that little circle spinning on your laptop there's this belief that somewhere in Uzbekistan, Nevada or Finland there are many Über-servers with satellite dishes generating and sending out data. "Data" means *gift* and these servers are gifting all this data to you in this unconditional act of endless generosity and data angels are dancing on the pinhead of your Wi-Fi. And this places you inside the universe of information and effectively of Being, but it's also incredibly anxious because you haven't *got* it yet; it's *coming*. Then the narrator has this almost Nietzschean counter-thought, which is: what if it's just a circle and nothing else? What if there *is* no connection or the connection was never there? What if it's just a stupid little circle and there are no angels? Also, when you're watching YouTube, you've got that grey line which shows the buffering in advance and the red line with the cursor which shows where you've actually got to and if the red catches up with grey, buffering kicks in. And this is also what my novel *Remainder* is about in a way: this décalage of experience needing to stay ahead, if only by a nose, of consciousness of experience. It's a narrative thing: the red line has to *render* the grey data, and this is narrative and consciousness, but if the two catch up with each other, then you're in this buffered moment where you can enjoy *neither* experience *nor* consciousness of experience; it's a narrative breakdown. So we can say this is modern or postmodern, but in a way this is also what *Hamlet* and *Don Quixote* are about. Don Quixote is trying to buffer his actions with cultural data. He's reading all these penny novels so that he can actually consume them and render them as experiences by re-enacting their moments, but he keeps running out of buffer space. And in *Hamlet* there are these continual connection drops and interruptions and interferences. This is why when you read Mallarmé now in the age of Edward Snowden and he talks about everything existing to become part of "The Book" and everything becoming legible, it seems to be incredibly contemporary. I don't want to reduce it just to the internet because it was more complex than that, but it definitely seems incredibly contemporary—even though Mallarmé says there is no such thing as "the contemporary."

Audience

I would like to know how important this moment of interruption is in the process of writing for you as a writer. If you read Mallarmé and Blanchot, for them it's so important that the moment of writing itself is the moment of interruption. When you write about the flower, you're killing the flower in writing it. And this is a kind of interruption which exactly corresponds to what you said about fiction, because that's the moment where the fiction starts. So for you as a writer, is this especially interesting because you are writing and because you're in this interruption all the time?

T.MC.

Yes, I think it is. You hear these famous writers saying that they have to turn the internet off if they want to write and that the distraction introduced by our technological media is all bad, but I just think it's wonderful: this drifting around Wikipedia where you start looking up Mallarmé (for example), and you end up on a page about artichokes or some South Pacific island five slips-sideways later. In a way these continual interruptions are a very productive thing. With Blanchot it's a bit more complex. In *The Writing of the Disaster* he talks about how absurd it is to even want to write because writing is the suspended beat where the disaster marks its time interval or its trauma. So writing is this kind of not writing. Writing is the thing that makes writing impossible. He says the same thing in *The Gaze of Orpheus*, or perhaps the same thing from the other way round: in order to write you have to be already writing. The space of writing can only be approached not by taking up a pen and writing, but by having already done that. It's this weird double negative which doesn't quite make a positive, it makes a triple negative somehow.

Audience

The figure of the terrorist crops up a lot in Conrad; and in fact you did an art project where you re-made the attack on the Greenwich Observatory in London that inspired *The Secret Agent*. When we speak of the figure of the terrorist around 1900, the attack is targeted less at state representation than at time, or more precisely the possibility of representing time. Disturbance doesn't so much entail exchanging one concept for another, rather than showing up how how order is produced, and thus how order can be disturbed, how we can fall out of the symbolic order of things. This entails thinking about disturbance in a radical manner.

T.MC.

In the wake of September the 11th, quite a few cultural commentators revisited Conrad's novel and said: this is the precedent; this is the first piece of symbolic terrorism. There are much better targets: the anarchist could have attacked parliament or he could have attacked the military, but he attacks the observatory, this building that has no strategic or actual power. It is purely symbolic: it symbolizes time. What is interesting about Greenwich is that zero degrees is entirely arbitrary. The equator has to be where the equator is because of the magnetic properties of the earth, its rotation and so on, but the longitudinal line could be anywhere. In fact, it used to be in Paris and then London wrested it off them in a political coup in 1880 or so. And if you go there, the zero degree line is actually written or cut into the ground; it is a mark: it is fiction. So I love this idea that the dominant order of time is already a fiction, and Conrad is drawn to it because it offers the chance of opening up another temporal, and political, and aesthetic mode, a vanguard one. In fact, one of the anarchist magazines of the time was called L'Avant Guarde. The attempt to blow up the observatory was an avant-garde attack on one fiction in the name of another set of fictions, which would not even replace it but purely disrupt it. So many of the literary and visual art players of that era were bomb throwers or sympathizers: from Pissarro to Anatole France to Claudel, all the post-impressionists, the Rosetti sisters, Ford Maddox Ford and Félix Fénéon. And of course Conrad is one of the pioneers of temporal dislocation in prose—prolepses, analepses, temporal jumps and loops—and even of a proto-William Burroughs kind of cut-up. The end of *The Secret Agent* ends with newspapers being cut as Winnie is going mad after she has murdered her husband; it samples all these papers and jumps forwards and backwards. So I see this as being intimately linked to a literary moment, and a political one; but not the type of political–literary moment that someone like Brecht or Raymond Williams might recognize. When Sartre told people like Bataille they should side with the Communists and replace bad power with good power, Bataille said he was not interested in that, the stakes were much bigger: he was interested in the replacement or the ousting of God.

Audience

The word "wait," of course, also evokes the word for the color white. At issue in Conrad's *Nigger of the Narcissus* is that you can't fake blackness. The hiatus becomes the thing itself; faking coughing turns into a real cough. This goes back to a well-known psychoanalytic point regarding simulation. Even if you are simulating a symptom you still suffer from the consequences of having this symptom.

T.MC.

I completely agree. I had never thought of the Wait–white elision, but I think it makes complete sense because Conrad is very attuned to—in an almost photographic sense—the idea of negative: the black, the white. Think of the end of *Heart of Darkness*, which is so much about race as well obviously: the blackness of the Africans, the whiteness of the ivory, and then you get this woman's forehead which is white with Europe's faith and blackness is coming all around it. We can think of photography itself, if we think of it in its old analog sense, as both a temporal intervention, a way of taking a bit of time away, but also as doing this by putting it into the negative: negativizing at the material level. Mallarmé as well is obsessed with this: the white stars of *Un Coup de Des* are negatively in the gulf of the page, represented as black dots. But I agree, white is spot on.

Audience
Regarding your discussion, at issue is not the possibility or impossibility of representing disaster and trauma but rather speaking *from* a moment of disaster. The disturbance at play does not so much involve the object as the space from which we can talk about disaster.

T.MC.
Exactly right: talking *from* rather than about—with the proviso that of course you cannot speak *from* that place; there is an impossibility. This is Freud's point: the moment of trauma is the one thing that eludes representation; the one thing that cannot be represented is the event. This is the same in Badiou or Mallarmé. As Blanchot says in *The Writing of the Disaster*, the event creates the entire field of the symbolic and yet, within

the symbolic, it cannot itself have a place. I think that is an overwhelming paradox that really significant literature grapples with and tries to speak from that place—which it cannot, but it tries anyhow.

Audience

The examples you gave for this recessional time were mainly waiting for one's own death or being dead already, but something that struck me about this mode of recessional time is that it is an interruption but it is in a certain way limited. What you have in Modernity, for instance in Beckett, is these phases of waiting for something but the wait will never end. The good thing about the recession is that at least it is in some way limited. But then you have these marks of time where you cannot say: is it now or is it infinity? Have you already gotten behind the end, like in *Endgame* or in *Waiting for Godot*? In Beckett you have this idea of being in between something but it might never end: we are in a limbo; the recession might last forever.

T.MC.

It's true: in Conrad you get the recession opening up and then it gets closed down again, so after Marlow has told his abyssal story in *Heart of Darkness* the manager snaps them all back into productive work; or in Faulkner's *As I Lay Dying* they bury Addie, they get her in the ground and then Anse just marries another woman, the very same woman he borrowed the spade from to dig Addie's grave—there is this recessional space but it is somehow contained. I guess that what Beckett is doing is just homing right in on that hiatus and making that the entire temporal field, and building a whole ethics there. "Was I sleeping while the others suffered?" is what Vladimir says when he looks at Estragon lying in the ditch. So I agree about Beckett; it is a really interesting point: it is never going to end. Perhaps that is why I did not really talk about Beckett. In a way Beckett would be the obvious person to think about when you think about waiting or a hiatus or a pause, and yet I didn't feel like I should include him in this because I think that something different is going on in Beckett.

Audience
Is the disturbance we find in Beckett's *Happy Days* a different type of disturbance then?

T.MC.
Happy Days is really interesting. This is a late Beckett play that starts with a flash and in the first draft Beckett had made it quite clear this was a nuclear bomb and the world was ending, but then in the final version he just cut any real reference to the world, so it is just a flash. Then you see a woman up to her waist in sand, Winnie, with her husband Willie attending to her; and in the second act she is up to her neck in sand—and there is not a third act. Winnie goes though a set of gestures: she opens her handbag and takes out a mirror, a toothbrush and a gun and she smashes the mirror and says "every day I do exactly this: I take out the

gun, I take out the toothbrush, I take out the mirror, I smash it. Tomorrow it will be back again and I will do it again." But in fact she is not actually right, because when she takes out the mirror the second time, it is not the same as the first time: she is re-enacting. If we all come back here tomorrow and sit exactly where we are sitting and say exactly what we are saying, it is not the same as now; we are re-enacting and if we do it the next day we are re-enacting a re-enactment—it becomes an accordion or bed-spring. So there is a kind of archiving and that is one kind of temporality going on in this play. Then a second thing is that there is the possibility of an escape in that play because of the gun; this Chekhovian gun that comes out. At the end of the play you see Willie crawling towards her with the gun and you do not know whether he is going to kill her or himself and end it—or not. That would be another type of interruption: an interruption to the pause that would finally bring about finitude. So I think in that play both are forms of terror: infinite hiatus is one form or horror and finitude itself would be another type of horror or violence. He leaves us suspended; a third hiatus between those two states of hiatus opens up. This is different from *Godot* because in *Godot* they kind of meet a resolution: they just know Godot is not going to come but at least they ask the page boy can tell him they were here—there is a Levinasian demand to be acknowledged. But *Happy Days* is more sophisticated in a way—and more horrifying.

Audience

What does recuperation entail after the rupture, which in your discussion recessional time involves?

T.MC.

I think there is a continuity between something like *Hamlet*—the out-of-jointness of time in that play and the re-enactments (he re-enacts his father's death and that is what causes the court to implode)—and Modernism and High Modernism and these other figures like Pynchon or Kathy Acker or Burroughs. But in terms of the politics of it all, I think it is very difficult to say that interruption is subversive—it is, but it gets recuperated. The punch line at the end of *The Magic Mountain* is that you get all this time off, homing in on death; and then it ends, the work of the world resumes—and what is the work of the world? Death. Hans Castorp recovers, steps out into World War I and is immediately blown to pieces. He survived for *that*? It is like a sick joke. So buffering is fascinating because everything stops, that circle spins, you get extremely anxious because that airline ticket you are buying is going to cost 200 euros more when it comes back, or maybe even the airline has just gone out of business, or your bank has crashed, or the server itself has blown up—so the entire time of the world and of your subjective agency is put on hold: there is a suspension. In the Nineties sometimes you would be watching cable TV in a hotel and it suddenly stopped and you thought: has a bomb just gone off in the studio? Has there been a revolution or is my plug not working? There is that sense of anything becoming possible. So that has very disruptive potential; but at the same time, if we want to get blatantly political, capitalism can recuperate everything. This is also what Naptha says to Hans Castorp. Capitalism contains reserves and generates a profit from precisely those moments of interruption, which is interest. This is what *The Merchant of Venice* is about as well. Even those pauses somehow get recuperated; but nonetheless it is interesting when another way, another rupture opens up.

Audience
How would you connect your discussion of recessional time with the violence that a philosopher like Badiou connects with what he calls the event?

T.MC.
I think that in "Action Restrained" Mallarmé does seem to elide and to blur the political and the aesthetic. For him, it doesn't seem like you can separate them out into different fields; and yet interestingly, while all his friends were running around throwing bombs, he did not. I think "Action Restrained" is almost his apologia for not being a card-carrying anarchist at the time. There is this sense of deferral and imminence and to-come-ness. Everything in Mallarmé is to come and that is what Derrida loves: democracy to come, the book to come—but it is not *now*. But also when he says "an event I have yet to name"—"j'ai toujours à nommer"—it has the double sense of "I have not yet named the event" or "I am always having to name it,

I am always only talking about that"; everything is the event and its imminence. It is very double-edged.

"Something that is not nothing"
Zurich seminar

Elisabeth Bronfen

Tom, our idea here was that you would give us a little insight into how you find your themes, how you use theory for your texts.

T.MC.

I'm not really sure what is and what isn't theory. I don't really know where theory stops and fiction begins. If you take someone like, for example, Derrida: half of *The Post Card* is basically an epistolary novel; it's fiction, there are characters, there is a character speaking to another character—even while he's conducting a "theoretical" analysis of Heidegger. I think it's very hard to pin down that border-line between it being theory/fiction or not theory/fiction. So theory wouldn't just be a reflection on something else which is somehow more integral; it's more fluid than that.

A figure like Lévi-Strauss is just wonderful in this respect: *Tristes Tropiques* is one of the most brilliant books and it's much better as literature than almost all of the fiction that was being produced in France at that time—with the possible exception of Robbe-Grillet or Claude Simon. When he describes the sunset for example; it's amazing. But it's also an undermining of any "natural" experience of sunset: he's describing it *and* theorizing it; the theorizing becomes not just part of the description but of the experience too. Lévi-Strauss clearly wants to be a great writer or to be a poet and doesn't quite manage. He always feels like he's doing the wrong thing, but in that very mode of "missing his calling," he produces almost a whole new field of discourse. There's that wonderful bit that I have my narrator reproduce almost word for word in *Satin Island*, where Lévi-Strauss is losing it and going a bit insane in the jungle and he decides to become a great playwright; so he turns his research notes over and starts writing an "epic" play on the flip side. I love the idea of the actual piece of paper: on one side you've got supposedly empirical, scientific, evidence-based research—although empiricists would say it's just speculative theory—and then on the other side you've got this attempt at epic art, which fails as well. Then, somewhere in the middle, if you could enlarge that physical piece of paper into three dimensions with a microscope, you would see this mulchy, messy pulp—and I think *that* would be the space of literature, which is neither one nor the other; it's this messy, unresolved *between*. This kind of slippage between not one thing and not quite another, this falling between two chairs or two horses all the time is one thing I was interested in.

When I started writing this novel, U, the character, was going to be a writer. I hadn't thought of anthropology, I just thought: he's a writer working for a contemporary consultancy, as Head of Semiotics or some such (this role really exists). Then I thought: do I really want to write a novel about a writer? It's been done a million times. Then I stumbled across the anthropologist as a much more interesting figure than a writer; but who is also to a large extent a stand-in for the figure of the writer. And I think it's significant that my hero is so compromised politically (feeding left-wing theory back into the corporate machine) because I just don't buy the myth of creative autonomy: this idea that the artist operates in some elevated space "outside," unbesmirched by society and politics and commerce and all the rest. Of course, we don't; you're inside the grid, you're operating in a relationship with power, always. So I think that's an aspect of what U, my hero, does in this book. Basically, theory, fiction and capital form the triangle around which this whole book is slipping between messily the whole time.

Audience

Could we relate recessionality to the idea of buffering that is so central to *Satin Island*—especially buffering the relation to narration? There's this idea developed by Peyman if we go into the text at chapter 7.7 and read: "We require experience to stay ahead, if only by a nose, of our consciousness of experience—if for no other reason than that the latter needs to make sense of the former, to (as Peyman would say) narrate it both to others and ourselves, and, for this purpose, has to be fed with a constant, unsorted supply of fresh sensations and events," which he bases of course on the idea of the YouTube lines. It comes up again on page 127: there's the scene where Petr is dying in hospital and he's talking about narrating events, and the impossibility of narrating the most important event—your own death—when you die. It seems to me that U is cut short at that point: he was trying to utter that it's a buffering problem, but he just gets buffered himself. I was wondering if this would really be a problem of buffering, or if it's rather a problem of the end of narration. The book narrates and then it ends: there's the last word, the last line, the last dot and it ends and then, there's a new idea of buffering which seemed to be in the middle of narration.

T.MC

What Petr is describing isn't exactly a buffering problem, it's a more Blanchotian thing about how to narrate the instant of your death. It's what he says in *L'Arrêt de mort*: these things only get interesting when I stop. The really meaningful stuff will communicate itself when I stop writing about it, but of course, at that point, who can read it? I think that's the problem Petr is describing there. But then he's thinking back to when he was in Berlin and the wall fell and even as he watched the wall fall he was thinking: "I'm going to tell everyone about the wall falling and how incredible it was." This happens in *Don Quixote*: the first time he rides out on one of his re-enactments as the noble knight Don Quixote, he basically plays himself a soundtrack in his head. He says: "When the book comes to be written of this moment, it's going to begin like this…"—and he starts writing it in his head. So in order to experience the presence of his present moment he has to detour it, wire it via its imaginary future mediation. And then it's a very strange temporality and he does this in order to be authentic, but he's radically inauthentic at that point. I was thinking about that a lot when I wrote *Remainder*.

But coming back to buffering, I tried to use that word and echo it in other parts in the book: when U meets the woman in the bar she's got a "buffer zone" of objects (cigarette lighter, drink, metro ticket etc) around herself; and when the Charon-like ferry arrives at the end, there are buffers to stop it smashing the peer and the dead parachutist is being "buffeted" by wind. It's not like there's one coherent thought behind it, so I can't really answer the question. I was just trying to kind of constellate some thoughts around the variations on this term, buffering.

Audience
However, you gave us a very interesting image, the image of Lévi-Strauss of the two sides of the paper, and then you said to imagine enlarging the middle. This idea of theory on one side and the literary text on the other side, or, one could also think of the *sujet barré* in Lacan—the barred subject. But normally when one talks about the bar, one just calls it a cut or trauma; an emptiness. What I found interesting in what you presented us in this image is that there is something. You called it "pulp," which is of course also a highly charged word in relation to literature: *pulp fiction*. Therefore, that's what I'm interested in: it's not just negativity; it's not just that there's nothing there, but there is something.

T.MC.

Yes, it's a material negative. And this is what the Satin Island is in the protagonist's dream. The same as when in *Remainder* the hero is trying to have his ideal moment of the liver lady frying liver and wants to smell it—what this actually creates is a massive mountain of congealed liver fat around the ventilator shafts. That would be another kind of Satin Island. This goes back to the material–immaterial thing: I think there is no immaterial; everything is material. Even digital culture is totally material. There are big black boxes in Nevada, Uzbekistan and Finland; there are wires. In *C* as well, radio is a material phenomenon; it's about pulses and atmospheric materiality moving through the air. Just because you can't see it, it doesn't mean it's not material. And writing would be a material practice—which is why U is so obsessed with the spilled oil. Particularly that moment when the black oil hits the white snow is a beautiful moment for him because this is *writing*. This is the moment of writing; it's ink polluting paper, or words marring the whiteness of a page. So it's another messy, fluid, material process.

Audience

When it comes to buffering in video images, we would normally think that it's just a disruption, it's just an interruption of the video stream, but it happens that when you have a frozen frame, you see something that you cannot normally see. All of a sudden you have a facial expression that you thought never existed.

T.MC.

Yes, it's fascinating. When the World Cup was on, I spent half the time just taking iPhone snapshots of the moment when the image froze. If you're watching it on a laptop it keeps freezing and pixelating in sometimes absolutely beautiful ways—bits of grass and player and sponsors' ads and overlaid broadcaster's text, all these blocks of color and movement collaging in every which arrangement—it becomes this really avant-garde piece of visual art. The interruption is a wonderful moment and it's not nothing, it's something much more interesting than the other thing.

E.B.

Would you say we're still in the modern period?

T.MC.

I don't know. You go back and read the *Oresteia* and it begins with an account of a signal network linking all of space together. At the beginning of *Agamemnon* you see this signal and then Clytemnestra comes out and says that Troy has fallen. She spends about two lines saying that and then another seventy lines or more describing every beacon between Troy and Argos. She's a nerd: she's describing a data network. And all this heroic stuff that follows, about vengeance and justice, is preconditioned on the fact of being in a communication grid. Is that modern then? That seems incredibly modern to me. *Hamlet* is also all about data surveillance and scanning private correspondence. I have a real problem saying this is modern and this is pre-modern. Also, I think the term "postmodern" is a real red herring. In his book *The Postmodern Condition* Lyotard says postmodernism isn't what comes *after* modernism, but it's an attitude of incredulity towards grand narratives. It's the interruption within the modern; the tendency to crack and split. So that's not really a temporal thing, even though clearly things are a bit different in different times.

E.B.

Probably it's the way one approaches texts rather than what they do. But I say this because I think there is a great epiphany in your novel. It's the same as in a Joyce novel or a Woolf novel: you can't grasp it, but it's just that something has actually *happened*. Something has changed, and he turns back to the sea. So, in fact, I see this very much in continuation with the people that you are invoking. I would agree that postmodernism is a red herring and even regarding what Lyotard says about the interruption within the modern: the modern always had that interruption within it to begin with. In fact, the early modern already has that interruption within it so that on some aesthetic, epistemological level, although there are historical differences, there is a clear continuum. Although, of course, how do we know? We're reading Shakespeare now through our eyes, so who knows how they would have read him in the 19th century. That's what I'm saying: part of it is definitely on the reception end. Nevertheless, I am taken with what I would call a quiet epiphany in your book, an unmarked epiphany, not an ecstatic, emphatic epiphany.

T.MC.

U thinks he has an epiphany about the parachutist—that he's "solved" the enigma of why parachutists are dying in series or parallel or whatever, by deciding it's a secret Russian Roulette cult, dispersed around the globe, whose members agree to randomly sabotage chutes, perhaps their own, to get an extra adrenaline rush—but the epiphany turns out to be totally bogus.

E.B.

Yes, that is bogus but then at the end of the book I would just say that something has *actually* become clear; it's only that it didn't matter whether he *went* to Staten Island to receive the epiphany that may or may not have been awaiting him there. That decision is both meaningless and in that sense also meaningful.

T.MC.

Yes, talking of the end, I more or less lifted that straight from Balzac's *Le Père Goriot.* The hero, Rastignac, goes through Paris and learns how dreadfully corrupt it is and at the end of the book (if I recall correctly—it's ages since I read it) he's standing on this hill above Paris and he looks one way out to the rest of the world and he realizes: I could just leave this shithole and turn my back on it and go out and discover new worlds. Then he turns back to Paris and he looks down on it and says "À nous deux"—"me and you"—and he walks back down the hill and goes back into the city. And I wanted that ending too. I think it's really important that U goes back into the heart of the machine with all his unresolved, restless anger. Staten, or Satin, Island would just be another city; it would be beyond, it would be leaving it all and walking out. It might even be death. But he goes back into the city and he continues to be this Kafka-like bug at the heart of the machine, the glitch. Even the machine operator is a piece of virus in a way.

E.B.

But I would say that that's a much more honest way of approaching the whole problem that you talked about at the very beginning—which is that we can't get outside the system. This is the Derridean idea that there is no "hors-texte." But there is actually something that somehow or other impinges on a text and there are moments when we recognize that. I think this is your point with the frozen pixelated image: there's a moment when the glitch becomes clear. In *The Matrix* it's that moment when the cat comes twice and you realize that this is the Matrix. It's not either you're in or your out of the system; we're always in the system, but that doesn't mean that we have no intimation or perhaps even perception of that which could be outside or beyond. I'm also thinking of Blanchot when he talks about "autre nuit," for example, as that which is beyond representation, but which can only really be thought of within the grid of representation. Great literature for Blanchot seeks to move beyond that; move outside, "hors." For him that whole idea of the "hors" is very important. This is what all of the work of literature is for: it's for the day; it's not for that other night, because we can't, in fact, fall out of the coordinates of the day. I could probably name hundreds of films that end with this idea of turning back, of going back into the machine. I looked at so many films where people move through the night, and at the end of the night, they turn back. They go back into the machine; they go back into the city. I was also thinking about Céline's *Voyage au bout de la nuit*, even though it has that emphatic epiphany: at the end of it all he sits on the bank of the river and says "I just want this all to be over," which, of course, it won't. Whereas here, U has seen something and he turns back. I think there's an honesty to that because, thinking about events, we grasp these events after they've happened as something that has happened, but not while they're happening. And that too means that everything is always part of the system. That's how I understand this buffer: we're just caught in that little ball and we keep spinning and spinning.

Audience

I'll ask one more thing about the buffering. In *Satin Island* there's a scene where U and his museum-curator friend are driving fast across a bridge in Frankfurt; and they see a crane turning; and the box suspended from its arm is moving down the arm—so everything is moving fast, but due to the relative speed and position of everything, it all seems still. Would you say that's a kind of buffering as well? The illusion of stillness only occurs because three movements in space are coordinated in such a way that only from this vantage point would that effect arise. So buffering as a conception of stillness when there isn't any: data packets are actually being exchanged and things are happening. Do you ascribe any productivity to the buffering itself? You talked about negativity a lot, but it seems to me that there is also productivity in the negativity. Would you say that's true?

T.MC.

Yes, it's a generative space. It's like in photography where it's the negative that produces the photo. It's almost the first image in *Satin Island* as well: a photographic image looming into view from noxious, poisonous, polluted chemicals in a dark room. And regarding the stillness, Eliot also talks about the still point of the turning world and this whole Romantic idea of tranquillity and emotion recollected in tranquillity.

Audience

Yes, but buffering is exactly not that. Buffering is recollection in anxiety. The Romantic position is no longer an option, nor is it desired I think. It's just much too self-conscious for our modern identities.

T.MC.

Yes, but with U's anxious recollecting there's all his whimsical stuff where he ponders a parachutist's death he's read about in the news, and muses on and on about parachutes while he's meant to be doing productive work, and even pins diagrams of parachutes to his walls; and when his boss, Tapio, calls him out on it and says, "what is all this crap?" he just makes something up, about how the parachute is a perfect structural illustration of the project the company is working on—which actually turns out to be true; it turns out to be a useful insight. And pondering this second fact, U cites the passage from *Tristes Tropiques* where Lévi-Strauss asks what a con is, and wonders if all of anthropology (and perhaps by extension, literature) is a con. Isn't knowledge a con? And then there's the whole question of stealing time and experience from work, from one's boss, from productivity and the general advancement of capital. Even walking down a corridor to his boss's office, moving through a blind spot hidden from the rest of the work-floor and clicking his fingers, and relishing that moment as it joins with all the other times he has clicked or will click his fingers as he moves through that same blind spot (like Hans Castorp waiting for his soup), U is entering another buffer zone or recess. I was reading lots of Michel de Certeau when I wrote *Satin Island*, and he talks a lot about the worker's small moments of private time grabbed back from the boss. But in a way that buffering is actually quite generative and quite useful. For example, Google says you've got to spend 20% of your time just wasting it, because they know that that's when the good stuff is going to come—which they will own. They force their employees to spend 20% of the time not doing what they're meant to be doing.

Audience

I think the paradox with the buffering is that once you see the epiphany, for example once you see the digitalness of a video stream that all of a sudden becomes much clearer when frozen, and once you recognize that as a moment to cherish or as a productive moment, it stops being that. Once you've realized you now have these free twenty minutes in which things happen, then it just becomes work.

E.B.
But isn't this like: you have to ejaculate now; you must enjoy now? How are you going to enjoy?

Audience
Yes, I think that's a good example.

T.MC.
The artist Omer Fast made a film about the porn industry. He goes on a pornography film set and just films what happens and it is exactly that: it's about this regulation and control of pleasure, which of course then isn't pleasure any more, it's just chemicals and bodies.

Audience
Yes, but I think the interesting thing is that you take the outtakes of a porno shoot, for example, and you turn that into pornography. You have people who are into the bits in between where nothing really happens: when the actors talk to each other or when you have someone like the fluffer girl who is only there so that the guy remains hard. You have people who are making that into the main subject. But that's the Marxist logic:

you can feed everything into the machine and make a product out of it, even the bits that at first could not be used; the waste.

E.B.

Warhol has written about that in his *From A to B and Back Again* where he talks about outtakes. He thinks the outtakes of movies are what things really should be about. I had the feeling that what you're also picking up on here is what the most serious of pop art is interested in. I was reading it in relationship to a project I'm working on regarding series and seriality, so I was very interested in the way the whole book keeps circling around: these people keep repeating things. They do it again and again and again and each time they do it, difference is brought into the sequence and you have the feeling that with each new repetition, it's not just that something was added, but, in fact, what was there before changes in retrospect because of the whole question of the repetition. What Warhol is so interested in with his silkscreens, for example, is that you have many images that keep getting repeated and all of them in a sense are the outtakes because none of them are the real image; they are the offcuts. So I think that in itself is an interesting aesthetic that one could think about.

T.MC.

U points out that as an anthropologist you're not interested in unique events, you're interested in generic events; in seriality and repetition. When U goes to the museum his friend who runs it explains to him that it's no good getting one fetish or cooking pot; you need a hundred, because then you study the morphology and it's in that repetition with difference that you can actually make a taxonomy of culture. This is very counterintuitive to a humanist or even a contemporary middlebrow literary credo where you're meant to be unique and have an absolutely unique remarkable thing. It's very much like Warhol: the boringness of just repeating the same with a difference is much more interesting.

Talking of outtakes, there's a very good contemporary Dutch artist called Aernout Mik. He's a video artist and his work is all about outtakes. He did a series which is very anxious to watch because he got hundreds of hours of footage of the Yugoslav wars and just took the outtake bits; not the horrible bits, not the bits where people are being shot or bombs are falling, but just the bits in between where nothing is happening. A bomb will have landed an hour ago or will land in another hour. It's incredibly boring—people are just milling around—but it's horrific too. He did the same thing when he staged a stock market crash: he showed the interim bit where people are just sitting around on the trading floor and there's all these chits of paper and the screens are all red and, again, nothing is really happening. These as well are the outtakes.

Audience
I just read *Remainder* a couple of weeks ago in preparation for this seminar and putting my impressions together now I wonder what importance authenticity

has. I think in *Remainder* it's quite important: he wants this genuine feeling of being *in the place*. This is not so prominent here, but, at the same time, there is this idea of using things in different contexts and there is still the big Project that is supposed to accomplish something. There are levels of truth, particularly in the part when he complains that some tribes don't make any sense at all and are too mysterious. There is the right mixture between understanding and not understanding, little pockets of mystery that need to remain in order to keep humankind going. And authenticity seems to be part of all of this, but I can't really put my finger on it.

T.MC.

In *Remainder* the hero believes in authenticity—he's a naïve hero. The hero of *Satin Island* is not naïve; he's a knowing subject, of course, as he's read his anthropology—whereas the guy in *Remainder* hasn't read his anthropology. But it still comes to the same thing because the guy in *Remainder* believes in authenticity and believes you can arrive at that moment of authenticity and, of course, he doesn't arrive at it. But then what happens is the accident: the radical, unplanned departure from the script where his bank heist, which is meant to be a simulation, goes wrong and the real jumps out. But the real is not authenticity anymore; it's a radical eruption within the inauthentic which is basically just pure violence. I guess here as well, it's in these interruptions, in these glitches and buffer zones that something else emerges—whether that's a vision of the whole fabric or what Derrida would call a space of unresolved difference or "différance." So in that sense they have that in common.

E.B.

I'm thinking of two other concepts: one is Duchamp's idea of that interval, that "infra-mince" where things don't ever fully come together but they're very close. And it seems to me that all of your novels are also an attempt to think around what Swiss curator Harald Szeemann, who did a big show here thirty years ago, called "Gesamtkunstwerk"; totalized art work. I think one can say that the whole 19th century moves towards that. One could think of someone like Wagner as an embodiment of that impact. But so much of the modern—call it the 20th century—could begin earlier with Baudelaire already. There's this desire for a "Gesamtkunstwerk" which brings together the different modes of perceiving the world and of understanding the world.

T.MC.

That would be the Great Report that U is meant to be writing throughout *Satin Island*—which he never actually gets round to writing.

E.B.

Yes, that's my sense. And it seems to me that if one were to compare this with *Remainder*, you would say you're getting at it from two different sides. The one guy believes in the authentic and he's trying to recreate that in these various architectural spaces. And what I'm interested in is the idea of trying to move towards that: constructing that, performing that, even if this inevitably always has to fail—that's Duchamp's point. That for me is the gesture of the modern, which, for all I care, begins around 1800, or actually, even with Shakespeare.

T.MC.

I completely agree. Regarding the "Gesamtkunstwerk," Mallarmé writes about "The Book." He says everything exists in order to be in The Book that is to come. One day "The Book" will come but it won't even look like a book. I was looking at his notes towards "The Book" and they're amazing: he's imagining rituals and hymns and sometimes it seems like Christians in the catacombs of Rome. And at other times it's a bit like theater, but he hates bourgeois theater so it's not going to be in a theater. It will be a book, but it also won't; it will be on and off the page. All the stuff that U is going on about, his musings about multimedia and performance and cult-activity and even revolution in relation to the Great Report, is just straight from Mallarmé. What would this transformative Great Report *be* and is it possible? At first U says it's not possible; and then an even worse thought strikes him, which is that it's already been done—by software. Every time we go on Amazon or Facebook, the networks of kinship are being mapped, our own likes and buyings and linking to others who we know or don't know but with whom we share liking or buying patterns, are being mapped, written—but we can't read it; only software can read software. It's this kind of Kafkaesque moment when he realizes that "The Book", like the plan for the Great Wall of China, has always–already been written and that we're already in it.

E.B.

For Mallarmé's Book to come, I would emphasize this notion that works in French: "à venir" which is also the future, "l'avenir." This is what Derrida does with his idea of the rogue and democracy. For him democracy is something that is always still to come. So if I'm trying to describe why I think there is an epiphany in *Satin Island*—the way I think there are epiphanies in the best of DeLillo's novels, while they are completely lacking in authors such as Paul Auster and Eugenides—it's because of this sense of a movement towards something which you want to reach, but which you also know you can never reach. It's this idea of something that is achievable, but is not yet achieved and should never be achieved because you want to keep that little bit of movement going. It seems to me that that's what you're bringing in here as well.

T.MC.

Derrida is huge for me and I love it when in *The Post Card* he spends his whole time trying to decode this post card he finds where he thinks Plato and Aristotle are having sex together. He thinks it's the secret of philosophy: Plato is transmitting while pretending to receive, and Aristotle is being ventriloquized by Plato, and it's all to do with transmission and obfuscation about transmission's networks. He basically spins the whole of Western philosophy out of this post card—and still then says that he's barely begun. He says that if only he could crack the post card that would be it; but then he realizes that would be horrific: the day there's a definitive reading of the post card is the end of philosophy, and democracy, and it's the end of love as well; it's the end of the world; it's fascism. This is why I hate what Quentin Meillassoux has done with Mallarmé in that idiotic book, *The Number and the Siren*, where he basically says, "I've cracked it: if you take the number of words in it and divide it by Mallarmé's birthday and my social security number you get the true answer, which is Jesus"—it's appalling. So I agree that this sense of incompletion is incredibly important and the whole of literature depends on the Book *not* being written.

Audience

But again, I think the danger here is of course that you start to fetishize the interval; you start to fetishize the incompletion, the lack. That's very much what one could criticize in Derrida.

T.MC.

Yes, it becomes buffer porn.

Audience

Yes, exactly. And that's why I'm still fascinated by this image that keeps coming up in *Satin Island*: of pulp, the messy "medium" or between-space that you envision as (for example) the middle of a piece of paper on either side of which are different types of meaningful writing. You would hold on to it and not call it a cut, or an emptiness, or a lack, but pulp; there is something.

T.MC.

That's the remainder; that's Bataille's base matter: the thing that's always there no matter how much you systematize it and think it; it's still just there, messy and unassimilable.

Audience

Talking about these zones of unresolved in-between-ness makes me think of Resnais' film *Nuit et brouillard*. The most interesting parts are when you see the surroundings of Auschwitz. It's made in '55 and he visits Auschwitz when it's not yet a museum. So you have these shots of the landscape surrounding Auschwitz and what is so haunting is that you don't see anything. And that is haunting in the sense that you feel you are responsible for filling in this void. The film does not remember for you; you have to remember because the film cannot capture what happened there; what it captures is really the in-between.

E.B.

I think this is what you, Tom, mean with the pulp.

Audience

Yes, something that is not nothing; it's in fact every-thing and that's what is really there. It's not something you can show to people.

T.MC.

U describes the pulp as "the middle, at whose outer edges the others hover like mirages." So epic art is a mirage at one end and science is a mirage hovering at the other and I guess the pulp would be another real as well. But it's not an epiphany in and of itself, because then the others would be fake epiphanies.

E.B.

It seems to me that you are talking about two reals: one is that moment of violence.

T.MC.

That's Leiris' moment where the bull's horn kills the matador or Ballard's moment where the car crash goes wrong and it's a real car crash. That's the violent real.

E.B.

Yes, and the other real is that material that is always there and that can't be brought into the grid but it's also not outside the grid. How do emotions come into play in all of this?

T.MC.

A criticism that some maybe more conservative critics or journalists have leveled about *Remainder* is that the character is so unfeeling: he doesn't have any compassion and he's just killing everyone or making them become automata in his almost Nazi control architecture. But then, when the man the hero doesn't even know has been shot in the street and the police take their photos, wash the blood away and reopen the street within three hours so that capitalism and life can continue, the hero is the one who goes: no, that's not enough; somebody has died here and we need to attend to it. And he goes back and back and re-enacts the death-moment—like people in the Philippines who nail themselves to crosses every Easter. Again and again, he places himself in the other's position, but not in some interpretative way. I hadn't read Levinas when I wrote that book, but I read him afterwards and thought that that's exactly what ethics is. That's another interruption: the interruption that comes back and snags itself again and again on that same glitch moment. So I'd say *Remainder* is actually a very ethical book—which is almost a perverse claim because he kills everyone. Levinas talks about ethics as happening at the moment where the bullet penetrates the skin—which is a very counterintuitive kind of language. In *Satin Island* as well, U becomes obsessed with a parachutist that he's never met. For him it's an individual—although it's not because there's one in Canada and one in New Zealand and it's happening everywhere, a series as you say—but there's also a kind of compassion for humanity there. And when he wants to become this anarcho-revolutionary saboteur, I would say that's also compassionate. It's political but I think there's a real passion in that as well. So I always try to displace the passion from one thing to some-thing else. Even when he's passionate with Madison, it's actually about the other thing; it's about seeing the buffering through her eyes. There's another bit in *The Post Card* where Derrida talks about a lover of his who was always very passionate, but who could only have an orgasm if she was thinking about someone else. No matter who she was making love with, she had to think about someone or something else.

Audience
That's very normal. Lacan would claim that that's ex-actly how it works: there's always someone else.

E.B.
There's M always watching Bond and the Bond girl.

T.MC.
Yes, don't get me started on Bond.

E.B.
Okay, I won't start you on Bond because, in fact, we have come to the end of our discussion. What in fact we did here I thought was staged buffering. I thought that for one and a half hours we were putting time on hold. Thank you for sharing this with us.

Editorial Note

This book is based on a talk given by Tom McCarthy at the Cafe Voltaire in Zurich on the 8th of December, 2014. The seminar the next day, at the University of Zurich, also included a discussion of Tom McCarthy's newest novel *Satin Island*. A second reading of this essay along with a further discussion of it took place on the 19th of June, 2015, during a conference on "Imaginations of Disturbance," organized by Lars Koch and Elisabeth Bronfen at the Technical University, Dresden. All the discussions were transcribed by Georgina Wood.

Elisabeth Bronfen